Weekly Planner

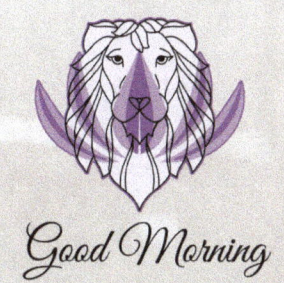

Good Morning

Published by Carol and Jacob Carruthers
The Lotus & The Lion
www.thelotusgroup.info
© 2022| The Lotus Group GA, LLC

Illustrated by Cocoa Twins © 2022
www.cocoatwins.com

For permissions contact:
info@thelotusgroup.info

WEEKLY
PLANNER

WEEK OF

MONDAY

TUESDAY

WEDNESDFAY

THURSDAY

FRIDAY

SATURDAY

SUNDAY

GOALS

TO DO LIST

NOTES

WEEKLY
PLANNER

WEEK OF

MONDAY

TUESDAY

WEDNESDAY

THURSDAY

FRIDAY

SATURDAY

SUNDAY

GOALS

TO DO LIST

NOTES

WEEKLY
PLANNER

MONDAY

TUESDAY

WEDNESDFAY

THURSDAY

FRIDAY

SATURDAY

SUNDAY

GOALS

TO DO LIST

NOTES

WEEKLY
PLANNER

WEEK OF

MONDAY

TUESDAY

WEDNESDFAY

THURSDAY

FRIDAY

SATURDAY

SUNDAY

GOALS

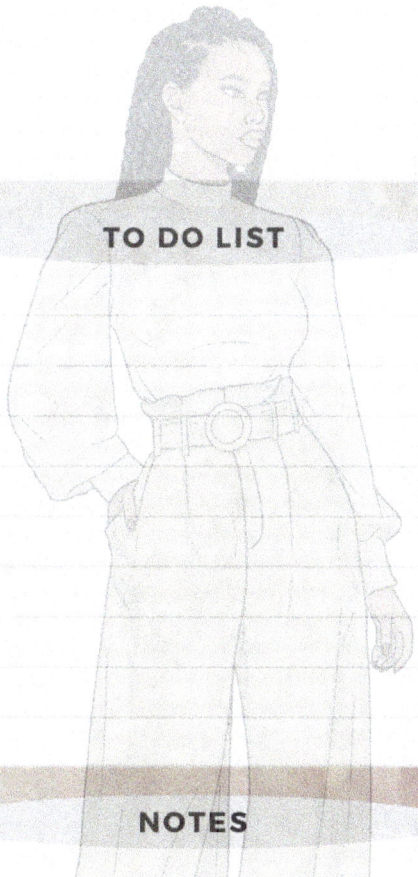

TO DO LIST

NOTES

WEEKLY
PLANNER

MONDAY

TUESDAY

WEDNESDFAY

THURSDAY

FRIDAY

SATURDAY

SUNDAY

GOALS

TO DO LIST

NOTES

WEEKLY
PLANNER

WEEK OF

MONDAY

TUESDAY

WEDNESDFAY

THURSDAY

FRIDAY

SATURDAY

SUNDAY

GOALS

TO DO LIST

NOTES

WEEKLY
PLANNER

WEEK OF

MONDAY

TUESDAY

WEDNESDFAY

THURSDAY

FRIDAY

SATURDAY

SUNDAY

GOALS

TO DO LIST

NOTES

WEEKLY
PLANNER

WEEK OF

MONDAY

TUESDAY

WEDNESDFAY

THURSDAY

FRIDAY

SATURDAY

SUNDAY

GOALS

TO DO LIST

NOTES

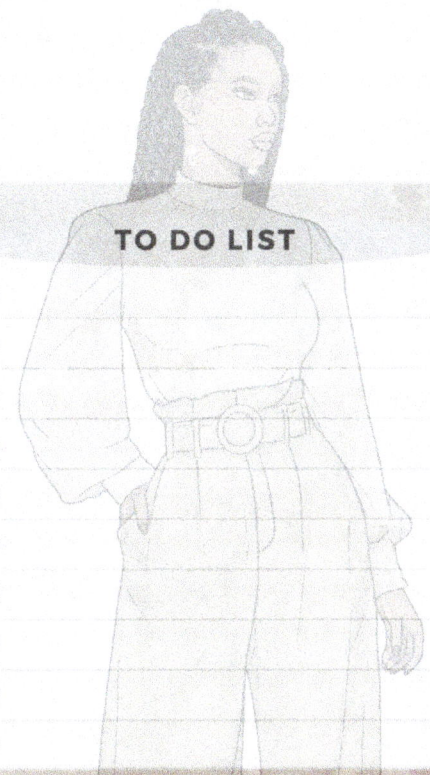

WEEKLY
PLANNER

WEEK OF

MONDAY

TUESDAY

WEDNESDFAY

THURSDAY

FRIDAY

SATURDAY

SUNDAY

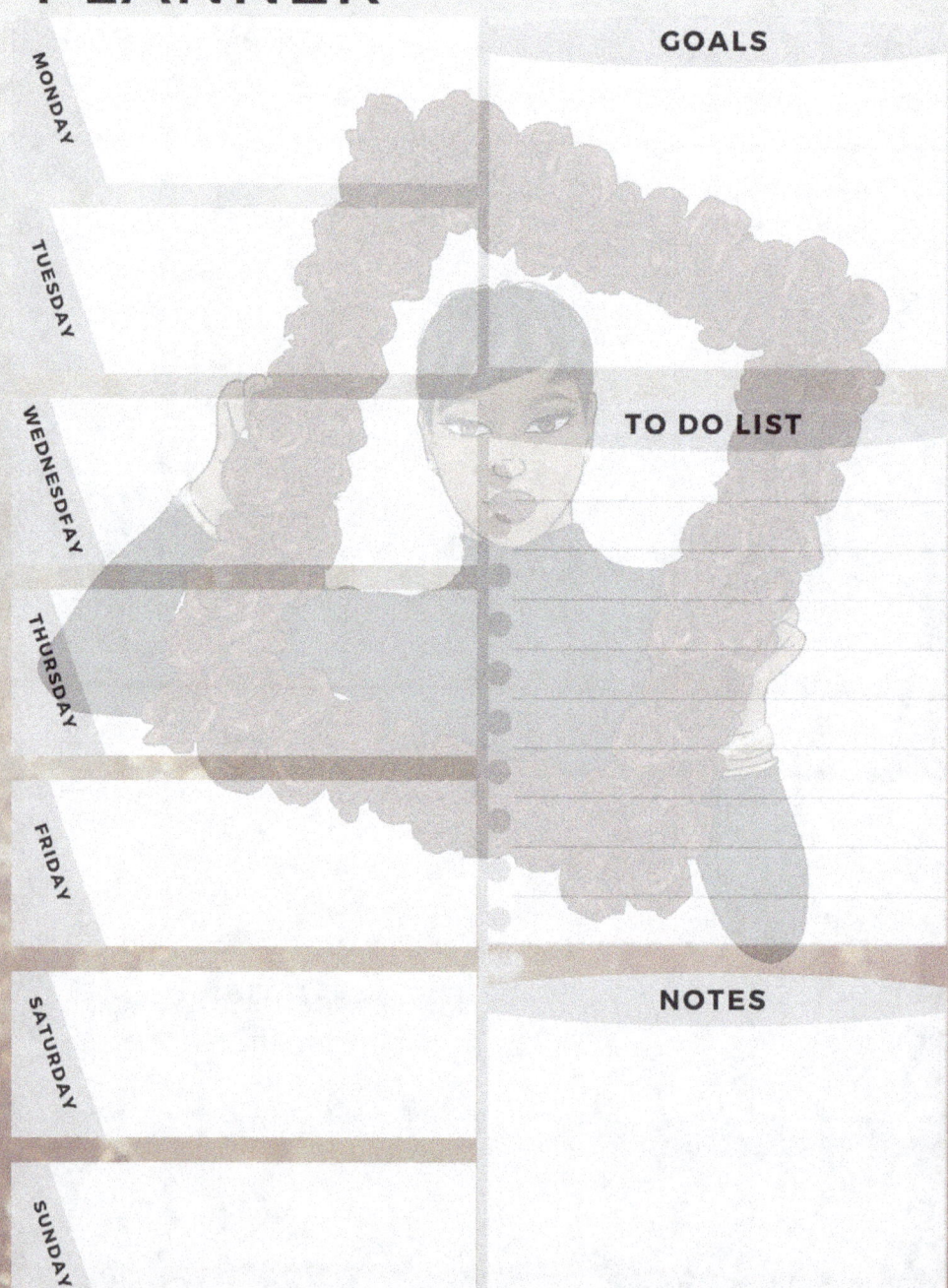

GOALS

TO DO LIST

NOTES

WEEKLY
PLANNER

WEEK OF

GOALS

MONDAY

TUESDAY

WEDNESDFAY

THURSDAY

FRIDAY

TO DO LIST

SATURDAY

NOTES

SUNDAY

WEEKLY
PLANNER

WEEK OF

MONDAY

TUESDAY

WEDNESDFAY

THURSDAY

FRIDAY

SATURDAY

SUNDAY

GOALS

TO DO LIST

NOTES

WEEKLY
PLANNER

WEEK OF

MONDAY

TUESDAY

WEDNESDFAY

THURSDAY

FRIDAY

SATURDAY

SUNDAY

GOALS

TO DO LIST

NOTES

WEEKLY
PLANNER

WEEK OF

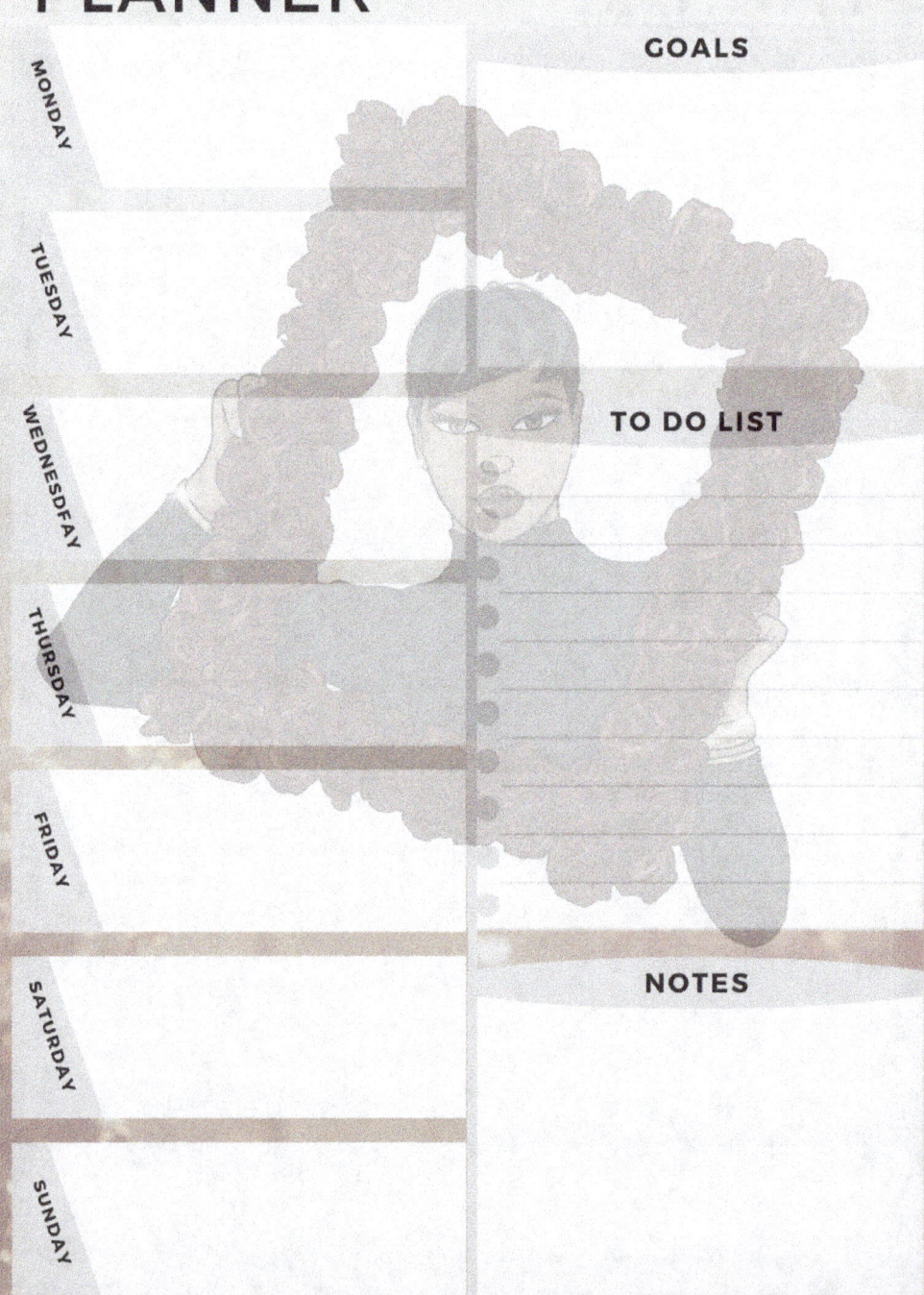

MONDAY

TUESDAY

WEDNESDFAY

THURSDAY

FRIDAY

SATURDAY

SUNDAY

GOALS

TO DO LIST

NOTES

WEEKLY
PLANNER

WEEK OF

MONDAY

TUESDAY

WEDNESDFAY

THURSDAY

FRIDAY

SATURDAY

SUNDAY

GOALS

TO DO LIST

NOTES

WEEKLY
PLANNER

WEEK OF

MONDAY

TUESDAY

WEDNESDFAY

THURSDAY

FRIDAY

SATURDAY

SUNDAY

GOALS

TO DO LIST

NOTES

WEEKLY
PLANNER

WEEK OF

MONDAY

TUESDAY

WEDNESDFAY

THURSDAY

FRIDAY

SATURDAY

SUNDAY

GOALS

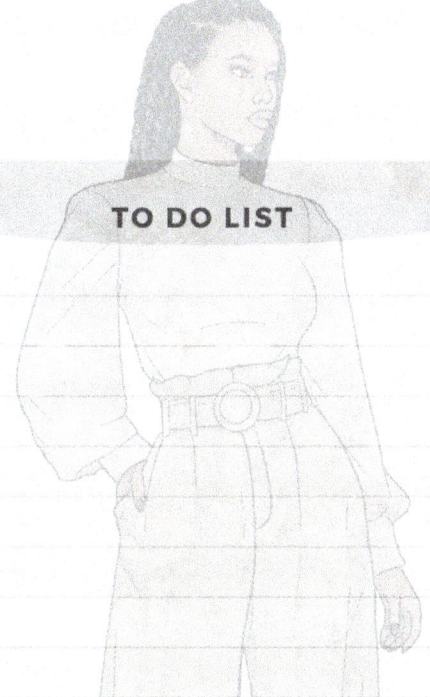

TO DO LIST

NOTES

WEEKLY
PLANNER
WEEK OF

MONDAY

TUESDAY

WEDNESDFAY

THURSDAY

FRIDAY

SATURDAY

SUNDAY

GOALS

TO DO LIST

NOTES

WEEKLY
PLANNER

WEEK OF

MONDAY

TUESDAY

WEDNESDFAY

THURSDAY

FRIDAY

SATURDAY

SUNDAY

GOALS

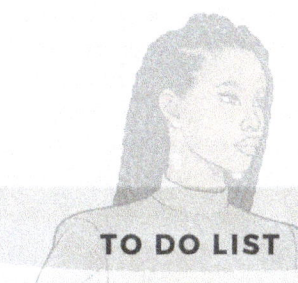

TO DO LIST

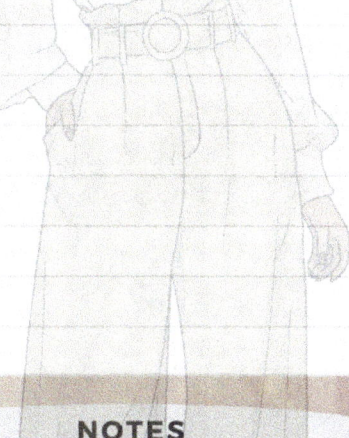

NOTES

WEEKLY
PLANNER

WEEK OF

MONDAY

TUESDAY

WEDNESDFAY

THURSDAY

FRIDAY

SATURDAY

SUNDAY

GOALS

TO DO LIST

NOTES

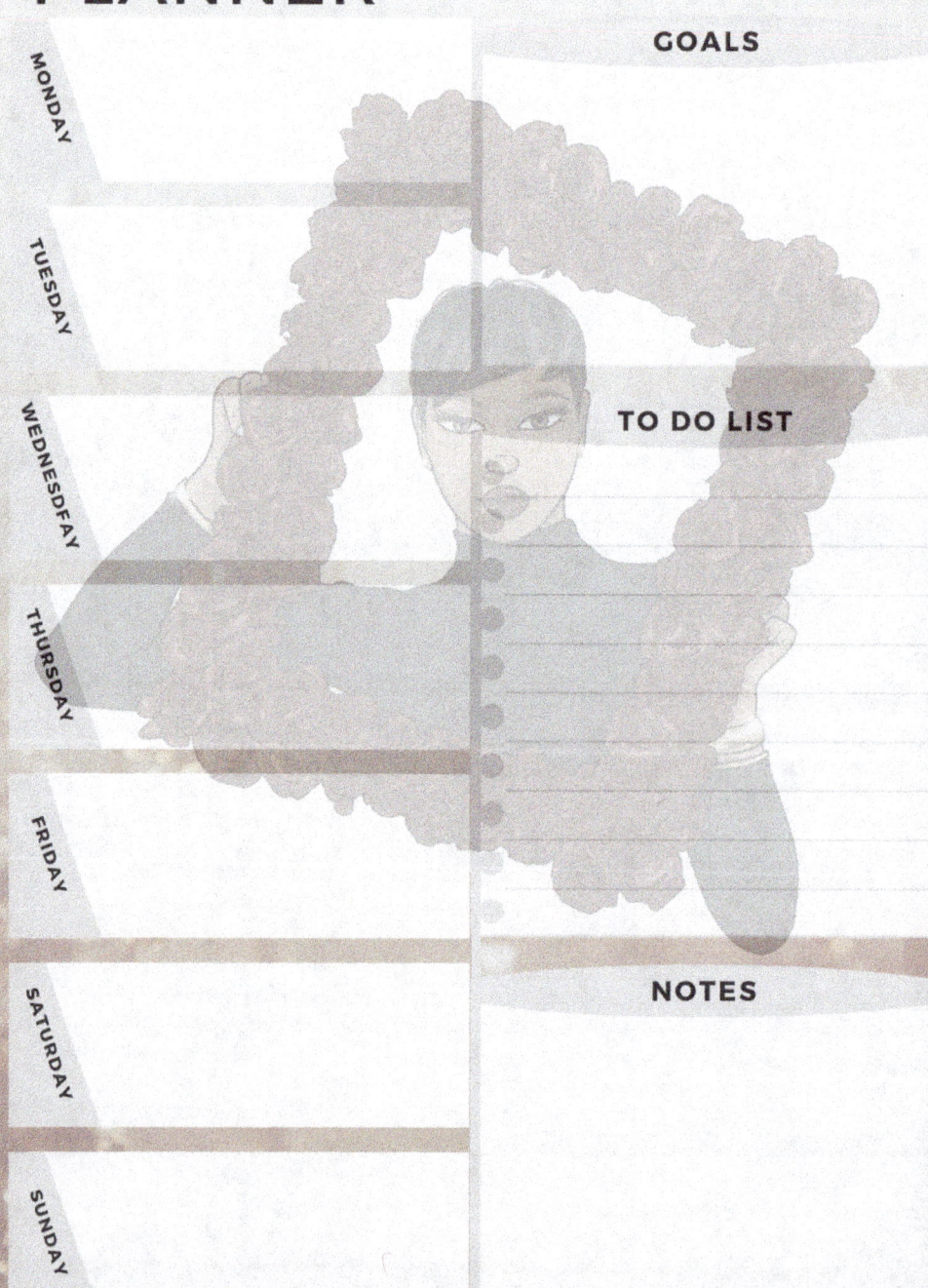

WEEKLY
PLANNER

WEEK OF

MONDAY

TUESDAY

WEDNESDFAY

THURSDAY

FRIDAY

SATURDAY

SUNDAY

GOALS

TO DO LIST

NOTES

WEEKLY
PLANNER

WEEK OF

MONDAY

TUESDAY

WEDNESDFAY

THURSDAY

FRIDAY

SATURDAY

SUNDAY

GOALS

TO DO LIST

NOTES

WEEKLY
PLANNER

WEEK OF

MONDAY

TUESDAY

WEDNESDFAY

THURSDAY

FRIDAY

SATURDAY

SUNDAY

GOALS

TO DO LIST

NOTES

WEEKLY
PLANNER

WEEK OF

MONDAY

TUESDAY

WEDNESDFAY

THURSDAY

FRIDAY

SATURDAY

SUNDAY

GOALS

TO DO LIST

NOTES

WEEKLY
PLANNER

WEEK OF

MONDAY

TUESDAY

WEDNESDFAY

THURSDAY

FRIDAY

SATURDAY

SUNDAY

GOALS

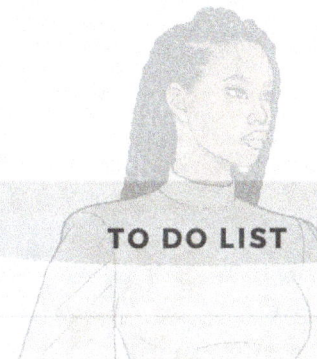

TO DO LIST

NOTES

WEEKLY
PLANNER

WEEK OF

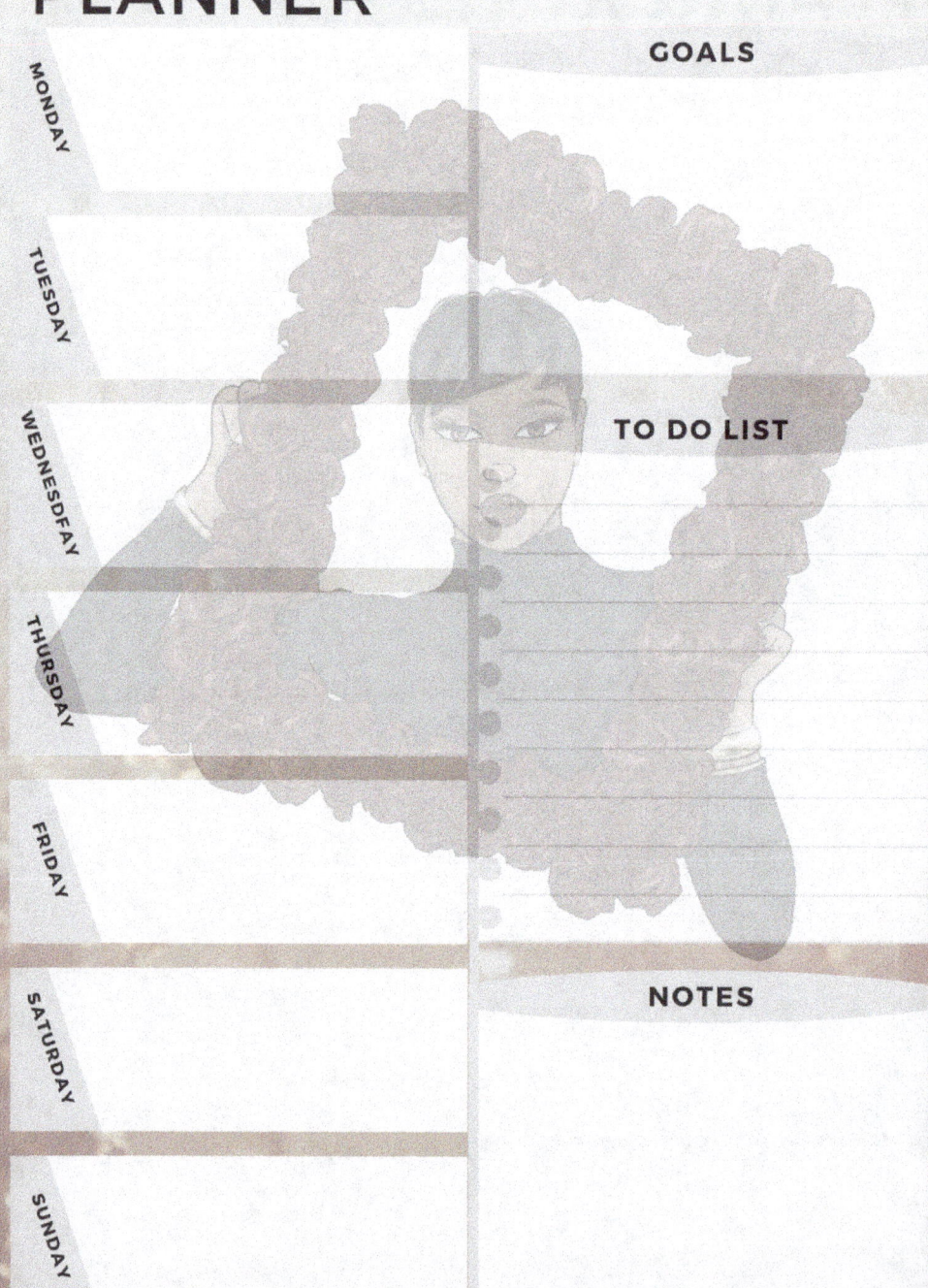

MONDAY

TUESDAY

WEDNESDFAY

THURSDAY

FRIDAY

SATURDAY

SUNDAY

GOALS

TO DO LIST

NOTES

WEEKLY
PLANNER

WEEK OF

GOALS

MONDAY

TUESDAY

WEDNESDFAY

THURSDAY

FRIDAY

SATURDAY

SUNDAY

TO DO LIST

NOTES

WEEKLY
PLANNER
WEEK OF

MONDAY

TUESDAY

WEDNESDFAY

THURSDAY

FRIDAY

SATURDAY

SUNDAY

GOALS

TO DO LIST

NOTES

WEEKLY
PLANNER

WEEK OF

MONDAY

TUESDAY

WEDNESDFAY

THURSDAY

FRIDAY

SATURDAY

SUNDAY

GOALS

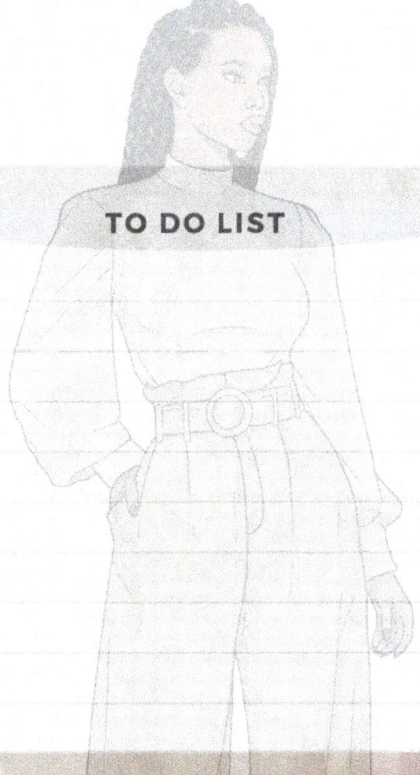

TO DO LIST

NOTES

WEEKLY
PLANNER

MONDAY

TUESDAY

WEDNESDFAY

THURSDAY

FRIDAY

SATURDAY

SUNDAY

GOALS

TO DO LIST

NOTES

WEEKLY
PLANNER

GOALS

MONDAY

TUESDAY

WEDNESDFAY

THURSDAY

FRIDAY

SATURDAY

SUNDAY

TO DO LIST

NOTES

WEEKLY
PLANNER

WEEK OF

MONDAY

TUESDAY

WEDNESDFAY

THURSDAY

FRIDAY

SATURDAY

SUNDAY

GOALS

TO DO LIST

NOTES

WEEKLY
PLANNER
WEEK OF

MONDAY

TUESDAY

WEDNESDFAY

THURSDAY

FRIDAY

SATURDAY

SUNDAY

GOALS

TO DO LIST

NOTES

WEEKLY
PLANNER

WEEK OF

MONDAY

TUESDAY

WEDNESDFAY

THURSDAY

FRIDAY

SATURDAY

SUNDAY

GOALS

TO DO LIST

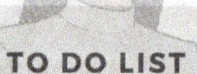

NOTES

WEEKLY
PLANNER

WEEK OF

MONDAY

TUESDAY

WEDNESDFAY

THURSDAY

FRIDAY

SATURDAY

SUNDAY

GOALS

TO DO LIST

NOTES

WEEKLY
PLANNER

WEEK OF

GOALS

MONDAY

TUESDAY

WEDNESDFAY

THURSDAY

FRIDAY

SATURDAY

SUNDAY

TO DO LIST

NOTES

WEEKLY
PLANNER

WEEK OF

MONDAY

TUESDAY

WEDNESDFAY

THURSDAY

FRIDAY

SATURDAY

SUNDAY

GOALS

TO DO LIST

NOTES

WEEKLY
PLANNER

WEEK OF

MONDAY

TUESDAY

WEDNESDFAY

THURSDAY

FRIDAY

SATURDAY

SUNDAY

GOALS

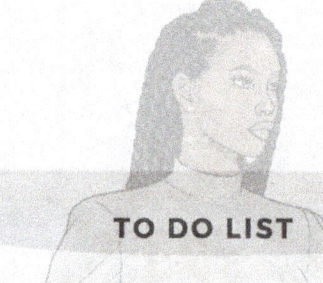

TO DO LIST

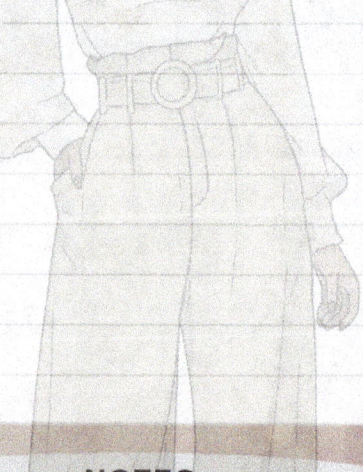

NOTES

WEEKLY
PLANNER

WEEK OF

MONDAY

TUESDAY

WEDNESDFAY

THURSDAY

FRIDAY

SATURDAY

SUNDAY

GOALS

TO DO LIST

NOTES

WEEKLY
PLANNER

WEEK OF

GOALS

MONDAY

TUESDAY

WEDNESDFAY

THURSDAY

FRIDAY

SATURDAY

SUNDAY

TO DO LIST

NOTES

WEEKLY
PLANNER

WEEK OF

MONDAY

TUESDAY

WEDNESDFAY

THURSDAY

FRIDAY

SATURDAY

SUNDAY

GOALS

TO DO LIST

NOTES

WEEKLY
PLANNER

WEEK OF

MONDAY

TUESDAY

WEDNESDFAY

THURSDAY

FRIDAY

SATURDAY

SUNDAY

GOALS

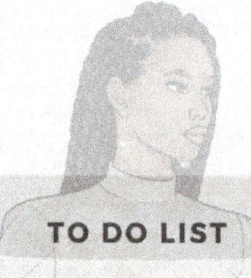

TO DO LIST

NOTES

WEEKLY PLANNER

WEEK OF

MONDAY

TUESDAY

WEDNESDAY

THURSDAY

FRIDAY

SATURDAY

SUNDAY

GOALS

TO DO LIST

NOTES

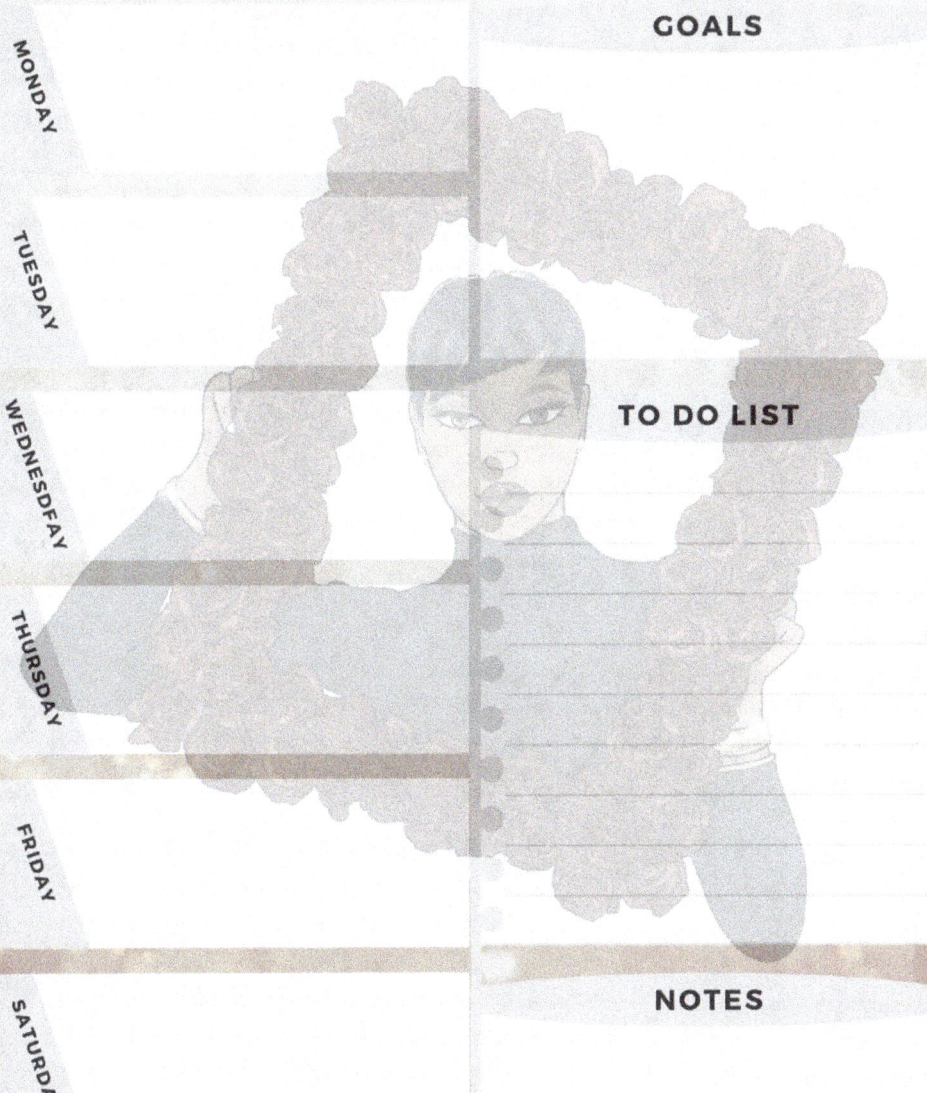

WEEKLY
PLANNER

WEEK OF

MONDAY

TUESDAY

WEDNESDFAY

THURSDAY

FRIDAY

SATURDAY

SUNDAY

GOALS

TO DO LIST

NOTES

WEEKLY
PLANNER

WEEK OF

MONDAY

TUESDAY

WEDNESDFAY

THURSDAY

FRIDAY

SATURDAY

SUNDAY

GOALS

TO DO LIST

NOTES

WEEKLY
PLANNER

WEEK OF

MONDAY

TUESDAY

WEDNESDFAY

THURSDAY

FRIDAY

SATURDAY

SUNDAY

GOALS

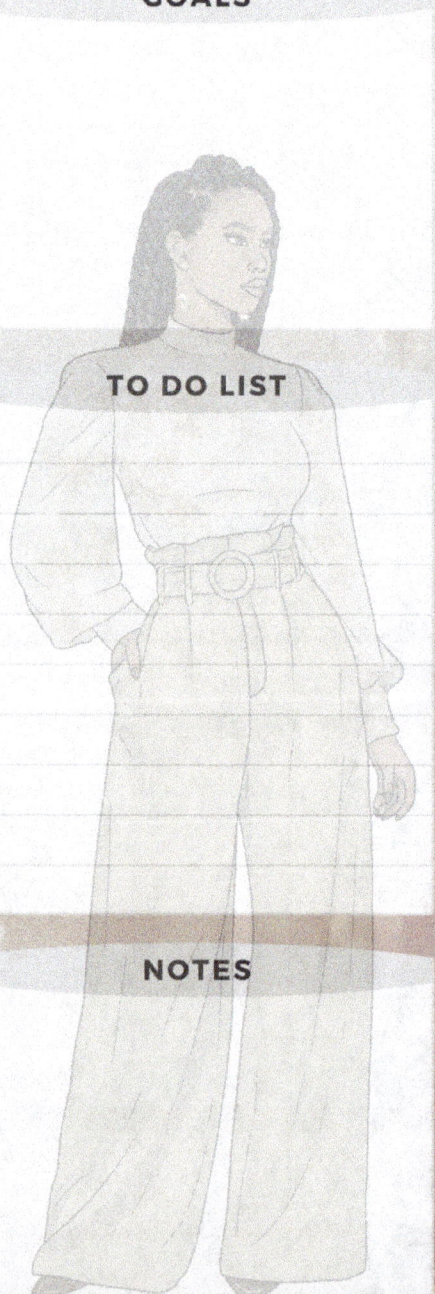

TO DO LIST

NOTES

WEEKLY
PLANNER

WEEK OF

MONDAY

TUESDAY

WEDNESDFAY

THURSDAY

FRIDAY

SATURDAY

SUNDAY

GOALS

TO DO LIST

NOTES

WEEKLY
PLANNER

WEEK OF

MONDAY

TUESDAY

WEDNESDFAY

THURSDAY

FRIDAY

SATURDAY

SUNDAY

GOALS

TO DO LIST

NOTES

WEEKLY
PLANNER

WEEK OF

MONDAY

TUESDAY

WEDNESDFAY

THURSDAY

FRIDAY

SATURDAY

SUNDAY

GOALS

TO DO LIST

NOTES

WEEKLY
PLANNER

WEEK OF

MONDAY

TUESDAY

WEDNESDFAY

THURSDAY

FRIDAY

SATURDAY

SUNDAY

GOALS

TO DO LIST

NOTES

WEEKLY
PLANNER

WEEK OF

MONDAY

TUESDAY

WEDNESDFAY

THURSDAY

FRIDAY

SATURDAY

SUNDAY

GOALS

TO DO LIST

NOTES

WEEKLY
PLANNER

WEEK OF

MONDAY

TUESDAY

WEDNESDFAY

THURSDAY

FRIDAY

SATURDAY

SUNDAY

GOALS

TO DO LIST

NOTES

WEEKLY
PLANNER
WEEK OF

MONDAY

TUESDAY

WEDNESDAY

THURSDAY

FRIDAY

SATURDAY

SUNDAY

GOALS

TO DO LIST

NOTES

WEEKLY
PLANNER
WEEK OF

MONDAY

TUESDAY

WEDNESDFAY

THURSDAY

FRIDAY

SATURDAY

SUNDAY

GOALS

TO DO LIST

NOTES

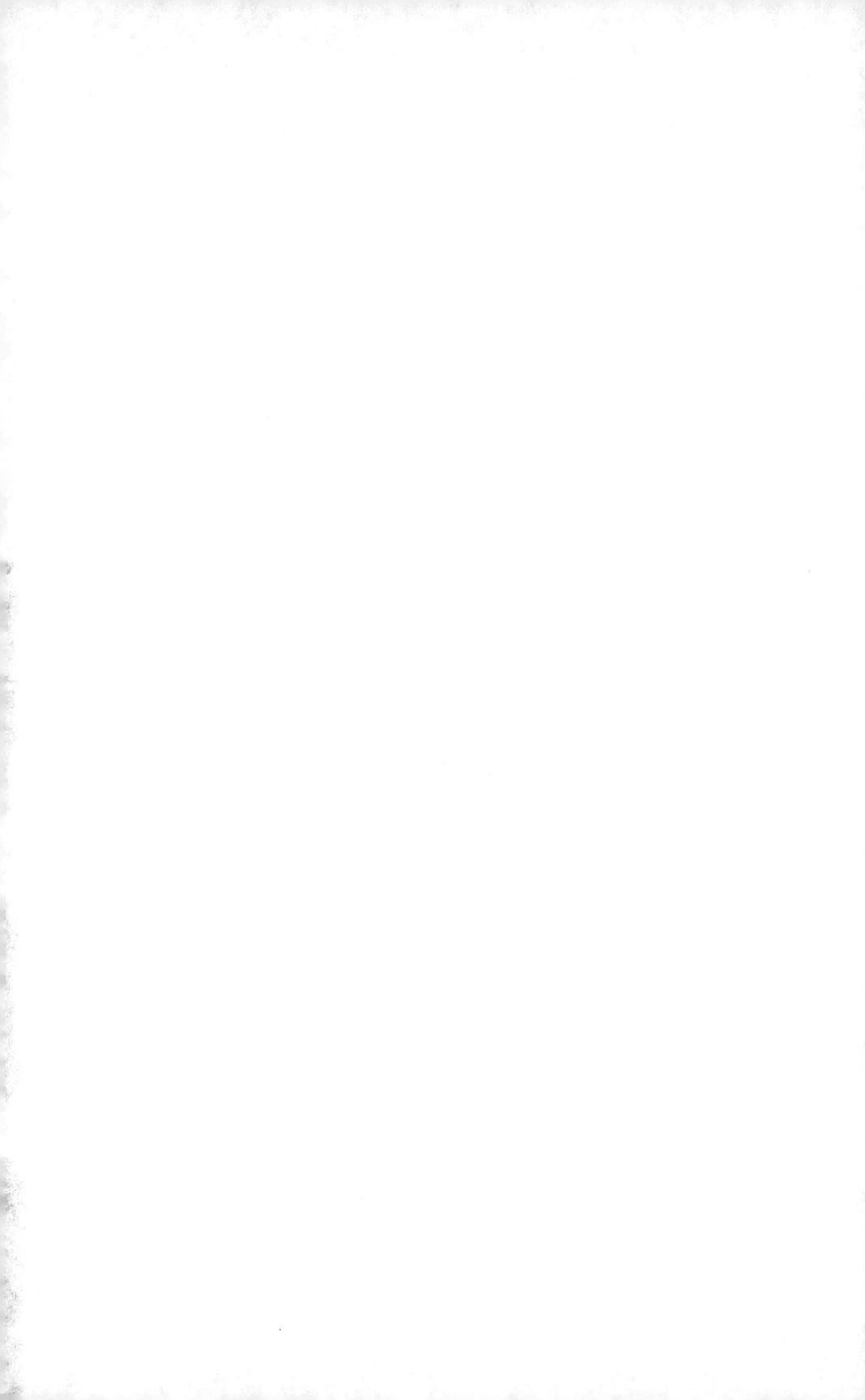